This book
belongs to

Published 2022

ISBN 978-0-6455592-4-8

Author Byron Guest

Title, The Cranky Crab

bobobooks.com.au

A rainbow
coloured unicorn,
has

1

amazing
magical horn.

A cranky crab on
sandy shores,
has

2

big red,
clicking claws.

Building with straw,
bricks and twigs,
are the

3

little pigs.

A kitten playing
on wooden floors,
has

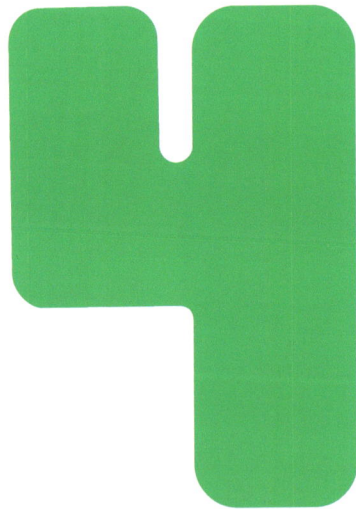

4

furry little paws.

A starfish crawls
on ocean sands,
with

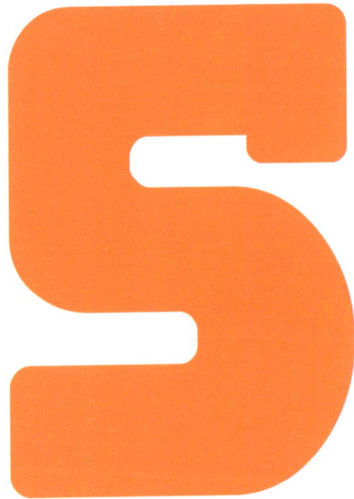

S

star shaped
pointed hands.

A magnifier is
needed to see,
an ant has

6

legs as small
as can be.

Upon the clouds
a rainbow stands,
with

7

brightly
coloured bands.

Octopus can swim,
walk and run,
having

8

legs is so much fun.

What does the clock
on the wall say?,
it's

9

o'clock
today.

Now you've learnt from 1 to

10

its time to count them all again.

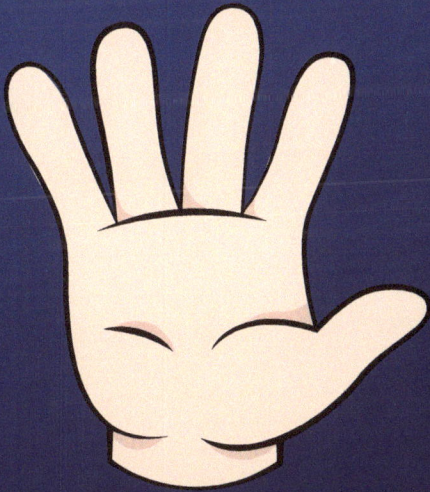

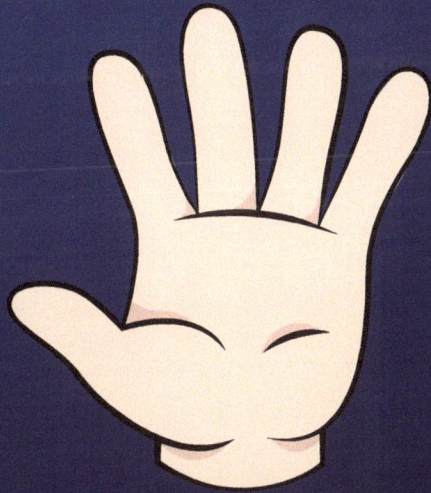

Colour in your own

UNICORN

Colour in your own

STARFISH

Colour in your own

TOWN HALL
CLOCK

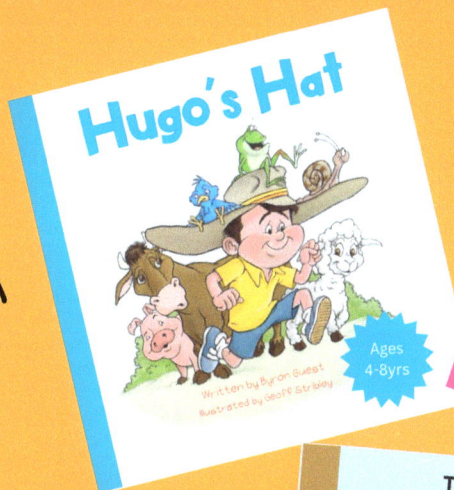

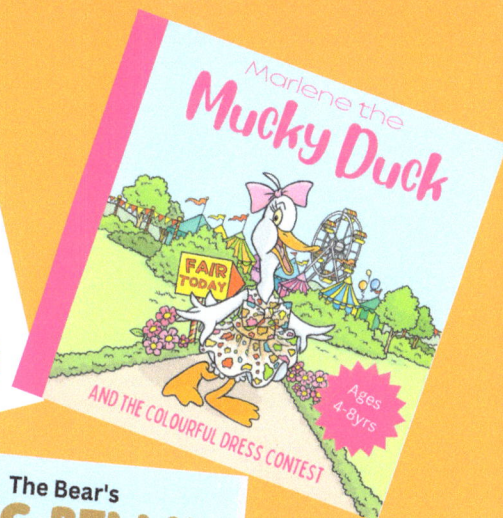

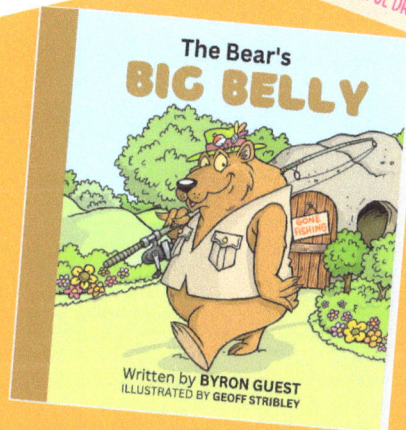

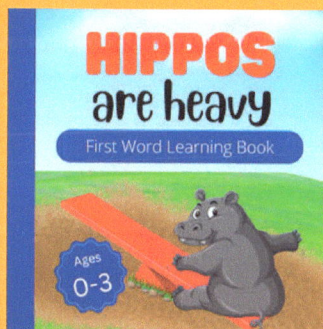

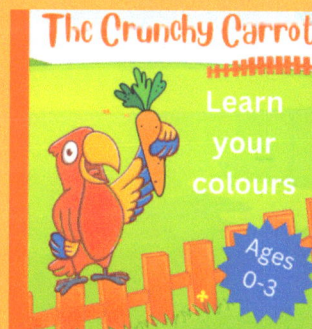

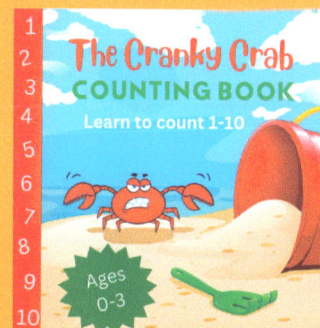